QUIT YOUR JOB IN 90 DAYS

By: Princess Fumi Hancock

Introduction

I was born and raised in Nigeria, West Africa, a country full of stories and emotions. I will share with you my experiences, struggles and how I handled all of it and became more expressive of myself, like I am today.

I hope that I may open up your inner self and help you express your dreams. Chase it, catch it and follow it. Never give up because nothing is unattainable. I am Princess Fumi, the daughter of the royal family.

Although I had many exciting things in my life, the thing that I knew I wanted to be since I was little was a writer. It was in me. The words always wanted to come out of me, as far back as I remember.

Back then, I made a deal with my father that I would come to America for a year to study writing. It has been more than 40 years and I am still here. I am still living the dream that I had since I was a little girl back in Nigeria. I wanted to be the kind of writer who changes people's lives.

My journey to get to where I am now was not sunshine and roses. It was not all perfect. I found myself living in America in an abusive relationship. It was a bad situation. It was nothing like my family ever wanted for me and it was the opposite of everything I ever dreamed of.

I lost all of the essence of who I was and all the things that were truly important in my life and that I really cared about. I even lost my home. I was completely and mentally out of it. I had lost it all. I built two thriving businesses and both of them were gone. I was left homeless.

I was at a point where I was inside my car on the edge of a bridge and I was ready to drive off the edge to just be done with it. I wanted to end my life and end the suffering. Fortunately, it was in that moment that I saw the faces of my children and I wanted to be there for them. They were the only thing I had left in my life that were giving me hope. I was thinking what their life would be like if I was no longer here.

It was something I found that I could hold onto and it made me step back from that edge. I was ashamed because it was an awful situation. I did not want to go back home to

Nigeria and tell my royal family that I was a failure.

The New Beginning

I left my home in Staten Island and moved to New Jersey. Even though I had an education, the only job I found was in a convenience store. The worst part was that I was assigned to the night shift and had to work inside the freezer.

There were times when I had to spend a long time inside and got to the point where I could no longer feel the cold. My body got used to it. I literally became numb to the life I was living and to the actual cold of that freezer.

I would bundle my children up, put them down to sleep and go to work all night in that freezer and later come home to my children sleeping on nothing but a floor - no mattress, nothing else, just a floor to sleep on.

I lived that life for 3 years and in that freezer I found myself beginning to pray. "God take me out of this life or show me a way out because I cannot live like this any longer" and as I said that prayer, I began to really truly look for a way out of that awful situation. It was at that point that the things began to change. That was the start of me becoming the Princess of Suburbia.

I left my job in the convenience store and decided to get a better job. Even though I worked my way up to a high corporate job, I was still not satisfied because I knew that, inside of me, I had a story to share. I had to write. I had to help women know how to come out of the difficult situations that were similar to what I'd been through.

I could not just work a job and make good money. I had to make an impact. I knew that if I was able to survive that awful situation, others could do it, too, and it was a story that I had to share.

Now I will be honest with you. I was worried because I knew that sooner or later I had to leave my job because sharing my story is just the start of everything else. I needed to do more than just share my story. I was worried that if I left my good job, my children might eventually go hungry again.

I was scared but I knew I had to step out. I knew I had to do it. I had to write. I had to learn how to package what I had been through so that I could help others have their breakthrough, so that I could teach others that there is a way out. That is when I begin to create the Creative Career

Conversion Solution, a way for you to be able to quit your job in 90 days.

Recreating Your Life

I became the poster child for all that I would teach. I used myself as the person who was going to quit their job in 90 days. I moved from working in the corporate world to being the person that I was meant to be and I did it. I kept track of all of my experiences all the way around.

The whole time I was aware of and made note of all of the things I was going through. I did this, so that now, I can share with you how you can quit your job in 90 days and fulfill the purpose that you have in life.

Since that time, since I made that jump, I have been a bestseller four times. One of my books was even made into a movie: "A Sentimental Value."

In order to be able to successfully quit your job in 90 days you have to start with re-engineering your life into a life of purpose. You have to position yourself in a place where you can be the person you were called to be. It is a part of your destiny to be that person that you were made to be and you have to embrace it.

You have to be the one to re-engineer yourself to stop

thinking and begin to start writing your legacy statement.

Ask yourself: "Who am I and how do I want people to know who I am?" Your purpose has already found you, so now it is your turn to take action.

I did some research recently and I discovered that 70% of Americans hate their jobs. Now, I thought that maybe that is just America. Sometimes things are different in America than the rest of the world and so I looked further and I found that across the whole world, 85% of people hate their job.

Are you one of those people? As you are reading this book,

are you wishing that you could just leave your job and start doing what you really want? Are you not paid enough? Are you being passed by for promotions? Or are you just missing out on the best version of yourself?

I am here telling you that now is the time to step out and begin to create a strategy to be able to quit your job in 90 days and live the life of purpose that you are made for.

You know that you just have to do it. You can feel it inside you - there is something calling you out. You might call it destiny. And if you avoid it, you are going to feel the lack of happiness and joy in your life.

Once we feel that call of destiny, we have to follow it because if we do not, it is going to affect us mentally and physically. It will actually show up in our health, in our eating habits and in all the things that we do.

Often we find people that are doing things like overeating or even taking drugs. They are actually just trying to hide from the destiny that they have been called to. So we need to embrace it rather than fight it and really go after the destiny that we are put here for.

When I embraced my destiny, the possibilities and the life that I was made for, my attitude towards my job began to change. People around me could see that I was happier. I was more focused at work.

The Process of Living Your Destiny

Everyone in my life noticed the difference and the difference came down to the fact that I was living my life with purpose rather than just taking life as it is.

So what are the things that you need to do?

Well first, you need to change your mental state. You need to embrace that you have a purpose. You need to stop telling yourself all the reasons why you're can't succeed and start looking for the all of the reasons how you can make it happen and why it will happen. You have to look at your cash flow and create a strategy from that. This starts by having a date of when you are going leave so that you just do not say to yourself "I am going to leave my job at some point." Instead, say to yourself "I am going to leave on..." Pick a date that will impact how you spend your money because now you are spending your money with a purpose. You are heading towards your exit strategy and in order to do that, you need to budget your money so that it can help you get to where you are going.

I know for myself that I could see what I needed to do to

make it happen. I had to create the cash flow so that I could be able to quit my job in 90 days and step out in my purpose.

Another thing that you need is help from others. You need a coach, a mentor. You need somebody that is outside of yourself that knows where you are going, that can help you get where you are going and as you go, that can point out other things you need to do in order to be successful.

After you have your mind right, after you have moved out of that place of stinking thinking, you have to write a legacy statement. You have to say to yourself, "What are the things that I want people to know me for? Who am I in this world and what am I going to present to the world?"

Then you have to create your exit strategy, with the expiration date so that you and the people in your life will hold you accountable for it.

Even when we put this in place, there will be projects at work that will get in the way of your exit, take up more of your time than you expected or be even more interesting than what they were before. Things like that are going to come up.

For me, I had a death in the family that impacted the journey that I was on to leave my job. Illnesses can come up. Bills that you have to take care of are going to affect your cash. But all of those things are the things that we can prepare for and we can expect to happen. You cannot expect that nothing will come up, but if you have a plan, you can then be prepared for how you are going to deal with those things when they come.

You can do things like letting your family know what you are doing so they can be on board with you. Then they can work with you to make your plans come together, as opposed to working against you because they do not know your plans. We have to let our family be part of our team.

Preparation is what helps us deal with the unexpected. I encourage you to have a positive mindset and keep telling yourself this: "I am never going to give up."

For me, I know what this is like. I tried for thirty years to be a writer. What I had to do was get help from my mentors and keep working at it until I was ready. I was always preparing so that I was ready.

In the end, the miracle happened in the exact right time. I define the miracle as the moment where opportunity meets your preparation. Be ready for that opportunity but be prepared to take advantage of it when it happens.

This is why you need someone in your life who is going to help you look at the things that have happened and the things that are happening in your life. You need somebody to point out to you that most of the things that have happened in your life are the things that prepared you to be right here, right now, so that you can quit your job in the next 90 days.

You may be seeing your failures as deterrents, but someone outside of you can show you that it is just a step of getting you to where you need to be in order to really fulfill your destiny.

Now is your time. We have to look at the timing of things and be ready to take advantage of the moment when the time is right.

We have to move forward from now on and we do this by marking the date that we decided to make the change. I want you to write down the date that you finished reading this book. I want you to begin to see that as the day that you made the decision, the day you are going to change your life. This is the start of you being able to quit your job in 90 days.

Leaving a Legacy Behind

Today is the day that is going to mark the change in your life forever. You need to sit down. You need to write that legacy statement. Don't think about the money that you want to leave for future generations. You need to ask yourself, who you are, what do you do, what do you want to be remembered for, and who does what you do serve.

I refer to myself as a vision midwife. I help people live their legacy. I help them birth their legacy into the world. You will find that defining who you are and what you do must be done with purpose and you will then begin to live your life differently. You begin to examine your life. You begin to live out the purpose you have discovered you are here for.

In this legacy statement, make sure you make it visual and motivating. Use phrases like "mountain shaker" or "vision midwife" to give yourself and others the imagery of who you are. Use exciting words that are visual to you, something that will bring pictures to your mind that are going to help you bring the best version of yourself.

Today is day one of your 90 days to quitting your job. You

are the hero in your own success rescue. I encourage you to be the hero. You can do it. I believe in you. Today is the start of your exciting journey of living your purpose and quitting your job in the next 90 days.